CRACK-UPS
UPS
A VERY SILLY
JOKE BOOK

KINGFISHER BOOKS
Grisewood & Dempsey Inc.
95 Madison Avenue
New York, New York 10016

First American edition 1994
2 4 6 8 10 9 7 5 3
This selection copyright © Grisewood & Dempsey Ltd. 1994
Illustrations copyright © Mik Brown 1984, 1994

Library of Congress Cataloging-in-Publication Data
Brown, Mik.
Crack-ups: a very silly joke book / by Mik Brown.—1st American
ed.
p.   cm.
1. Riddles, Juvenile.   2. Animals—Juvenile humor.   [1. Riddles.
2. Jokes.]   I. Title.
PN6371.5.B77   1994
818′.5402—dc20   93–28644 CIP   AC

ISBN 1-85697-930-X

Edited by Sian Hardy
Printed in Great Britain

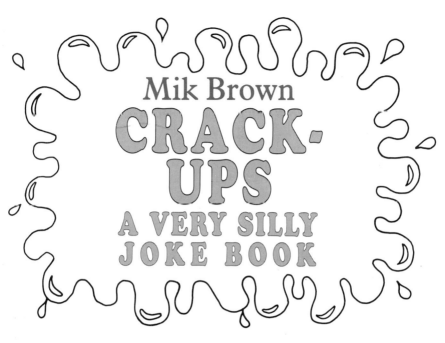

Mik Brown
CRACK-UPS
A VERY SILLY JOKE BOOK

Kingfisher Books

NEW YORK

Why did the elephant paint his toenails red?

So he could hide in the cherry tree.

Why does an elephant wear sneakers?

So that he can sneak up on mice.

What time is it when an elephant sits on the fence?

Time to fix the fence.

How do you know when there's an elephant under your bed?

When your nose touches the ceiling.

What's the difference between an elephant and a flea?

An elephant can have fleas, but a flea can't have elephants.

Why were the elephants thrown out of the swimming pool?

Because they couldn't keep their trunks up.

How do you know when there's an elephant in the refrigerator?

When you can't shut the door.

THUD!

What do you get if you cross an elephant with a kangaroo?

Great big holes all over Australia.

What do you call an elephant that flies?

A jumbo jet.

**Why did the elephant paint
himself different colors?**

Because he wanted
to hide in the crayon box.

**How does an elephant
get down from a tree?**

He sits on a leaf and
waits for the fall.

**What is as big as an
elephant but doesn't
weigh anything?**

An elephant's shadow.

**Why are elephants
so wrinkled?**

Have you ever tried ironing one?

One snake said to another:

"Are we supposed to be poisonous?"
"Why?"
"Because I've just bitten my lip."

**What do you get if
you cross a snake
with a magician?**

Abra da cobra.

**What's green and
slimy and goes *hith*?**

A snake with a lisp.

What do polar bears have for lunch?

Ice burgers.

What gets wet as it dries?

A towel.

What animal do you look like in the bath?

A little bear.

What's white outside, green inside, and hops?

A frog sandwich.

**Spell "mousetrap"
in three letters.**

C-A-T.

FREDA: "Will I be able to read with these glasses?"

FRED: "You certainly will."

FREDA: "That's good. I couldn't before."

Where do you take a frog with bad eyesight?

To the hoptician.

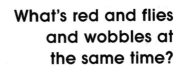

What's red and flies and wobbles at the same time?

A jellocopter.

What's green and can jump a mile a minute?

A frog with hiccups.

**What's scaly,
has a hard shell,
and bounces?**

A tortoise on a
pogo stick.

BOING!
BOING!

**What's black and shiny,
lives in trees, and is
very dangerous?**

A crow with a machine gun.

**What was the tortoise doing
on the freeway?**

About 150 inches an hour.

A giraffe, an elephant, a camel, a bear, a pig, and a frog, two mice, and a snake all sheltered under one umbrella; how many got wet?

None, it wasn't raining.

Why are goldfish red?

The water makes them rusty.

What did the sardine call the submarine?

A can of people.

TEACHER: "You should have been here at 9 o'clock."

PUPIL: "Why, what happened?"

What kind of noise annoys an oyster?

A noisy noise annoys an oyster.

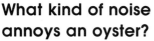

What's yellow and highly dangerous?

Shark-infested banana pudding.

What do you get from a bad-tempered shark?

As far away as possible.

What do you call someone with a seagull on his head?

Cliff.

What do you get if you cross a snowman with a tiger?

Frostbite.

GRRRR!

What's yellow and black with red spots?

A leopard with the measles.

LION: "You're a cheater!"

CHEETAH: "You're lion!"

Why is it hard for leopards to hide?

Because they're always spotted.

I CAN SEE YOU!

If athletes get athlete's foot, what do astronauts get?

Missile-toe.

What do astronauts eat for lunch?

Launch-meat sandwiches.

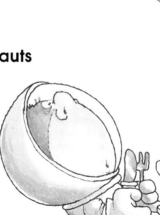

ZOOM

What do you call a mad astronaut?

An astronut.

How do you get a baby astronaut to go to sleep?

You rock-et.

SPLOP!

What did the astronaut see in his frying pan?

An unidentified frying object.

What do you give a sick pig?

Oinkment.

What kind of tie does a pig wear?

A pigsty.

Why is getting up in the morning like a pig's tail?

Because it's twirly (too early).

One camel said to another:

> "Did you know the cleverest camel in
>   the desert was deaf?"
> "Really—who is it?"
> "Pardon?"

**What was the name of
the camel without a hump?**

Humphrey.

**What animal with two humps
can be found at
the North Pole?**

A lost camel.

"Waiter, this soup tastes funny."

"Then why aren't you laughing?"

"Waiter, what's this fly doing in my soup?"

"Looks like it's learning to swim, sir."

"Waiter, there's a small slug on this lettuce."

"Sorry, sir, shall I get you a bigger one?"

"Waiter, there's a mouse in my hamburger."

"Don't shout, sir, or everyone will want one."

"Waiter, do you have frogs' legs?"

"No, sir, I've always walked like this."

"Waiter, there's a caterpillar on my salad."

"Don't worry, sir, there's no extra charge."

"Waiter, there's a fly in my soup."

"Don't worry, sir, that spider on your bread will soon get rid of it."

"Waiter, your thumb is in my soup."

"That's okay, ma'am, it's not hot."

"Waiter, this coffee is terrible — it tastes like earth!"

"Yes, sir, it was ground yesterday."

"Waiter, is there soup on the menu?"

"No, ma'am, I wiped it off."

"Waiter, this egg is bad."

"Don't blame me, ma'am, I only laid the table."

"Waiter, bring me something to eat, and make it snappy."

"How about a crocodile sandwich, sir."

What did the pony say when he coughed?

"Excuse me, I'm just a little horse."

What did the hungry donkey say when it had only thistles to eat?

"Thist-le have to do."

Who always goes to bed with shoes on?

A horse.

**How do you start
a flea race?**

1, 2, flea, go.

**What did the earwig say
when it fell off the cliff?**

"'Ere we go."

What lies down a hundred feet in the air?

A centipede.

What bee can never be understood?

A mumble-bee.

Why do bees hum?

Because they don't know the words.

What is the biggest ant?

An elephant.

How can you tell which end of a worm is which?

Tickle its middle and see which end smiles.

When did the fly fly?

When the spider spied her.

When the dentist put his fingers in the crocodile's mouth to see how many teeth it had, what did the crocodile do?

It closed its mouth to see how many fingers the dentist had.

What's a crocodile's favorite card game?

Snap.

What do you call a sick alligator?

An illigator.

What's the difference between a crocodile and a mailbox?

If you don't know, watch out next time you mail a letter.

Have you heard the joke about the watermelon?

It's pitiful.

What's green and dangerous and good at arithmetic?

A crocodile with a calculator.

How do you tell a rabbit from a gorilla?

A rabbit doesn't look like a gorilla.

What is a twip?

A twip is what a wabbit makes when he wides a twain.

What do you get if you pour hot water down a rabbit-hole?

Hot-cross bunnies.

"If I give you three rabbits . . .

. . . and then I give you two rabbits . .

. . . how many rabbits will you have?"

"Six."   "Six?"

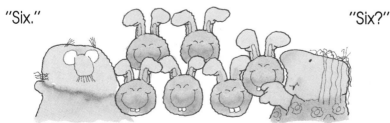

"Yes, I've got one already."

How do you stop a skunk from smelling?

Hold its nose.

**What do you get
if you cross a
bear with a skunk?**

Winnie the Pooh.

**What do skunks have that no
other animals have?**

Baby skunks.

What's black and white and very noisy?

A skunk with a drum set.

What's black and white and has sixteen wheels?

A zebra on roller skates.

What do you call a gorilla wearing headphones?

Anything you like, he can't hear you.

YELL!

Why does a monkey scratch himself?

Because he's the only one who knows where it itches.

How do you catch a monkey?

Hang upside down in a tree and make a noise like a banana.

Why are monsters forgetful?

Because everything you tell them goes in one ear and out the others.

Why did the monster knit herself three socks?

Because she grew another foot.

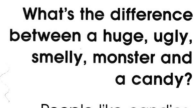

What's the difference between a huge, ugly, smelly, monster and a candy?

People like candies.

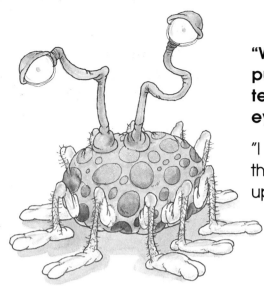

"What has a purple-spotted body, ten hairy legs, and big eyes on stalks?"

"I don't know, but there's one crawling up your leg."

What do you say when you meet a two-headed monster?

"Hello, hello!"

What is the best way to speak to a monster?

From far, far away.

What's big, red, and prickly, has three eyes, and eats rocks?

A big, red, prickly, three-eyed rock-eater.

How does a monster count to fifteen?

On its fingers.

"Doctor, doctor, I feel like a bell."

"Take these and,
if they don't work,
give me a ring."

**"Doctor, doctor, I keep thinking
I'm a trash can."**

"Don't talk garbage."

**"Doctor, doctor, I keep
forgetting things."**

"When did this start
happening?"

**"When did what start
happening?"**

Why didn't the skeleton go to the party?

It had no-body to go with.

PATIENT: "Will my chicken pox get better?"

DOCTOR: "I don't like making rash promises."

DOCTOR: "Did you drink your orange juice after your bath?"

PATIENT: "After drinking the bath, I didn't have much room for the orange juice."

"Doctor, doctor, my hair keeps falling out. Can you give me something to keep it in?"

"How about a paper bag?"

"Doctor, doctor, I feel like an apple."

"Come over here, I won't bite you."

Doctor, doctor, I keep thinking I'm invisible."

"Who said that?"

"Doctor, doctor, I feel like a pair of curtains."

"Pull yourself together."

"Doctor, doctor, I've got a terrible sore throat."

"Go over to the window and stick your tongue out."

"Will that help my throat?"

"No, I just don't like the man next door."

"Doctor, doctor, everybody ignores me."

"Next, please."

"If I had eight porcupines in one hand and seven porcupines in the other, what would I have?"

"Big hands."

Why did the porcupine wear red boots?

Because his brown ones were being repaired.

**What did the
porcupine say
to the cactus?**

"Is that you, Mama?"

**Where would you find
a prehistoric cow?**

In a moo-seum.

**What do you call a cow that
eats your grass?**

A lawn moo-er!

**Which cows have
the shortest legs?**

The smallest ones.

Why did the cow go over the hill?

Because it couldn't go under it.

Where do cows go on a Saturday night?

To the moo-vies.

What goes OOM OOM?

A cow walking backwards.

**What do you call a bull
asleep on the ground?**

A bulldozer.

FIRST COW: "Moo."

SECOND COW: "Baa-a-a."

FIRST COW: "What do you mean 'Baa-a-a'?"

SECOND COW: "I'm learning a foreign
language."

MOOO!

BAAA!

HOW NOW BROWN SHEEP.

**What's white,
has four legs,
and a trunk?**

A mouse going
on vacation.

**What do angry mice send each other
at Christmas?**

Cross-mouse cards.

**What's brown,
has four legs,
and a trunk?**

A mouse coming
back from vacation.

What do mice do in the daytime?

Mousework.

How can you tell one cat from another?

Look them up in a catalog.

What's gray, has four legs, and weighs one-and-a-half pounds?

A fat mouse.

What has the head of a cat, the tail of a cat, but is not a cat?

A kitten.

What works in a circus, does somersaults, and meows?

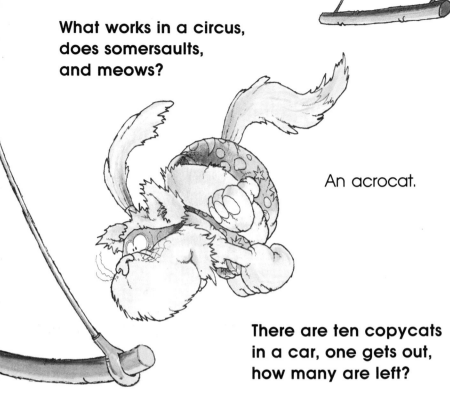

An acrocat.

There are ten copycats in a car, one gets out, how many are left?

None.

Why do cats have furry coats?

Because they'd look silly in plastic ones.

How do you stop your dog barking in the house?

Put it outside.

"Your dog's been chasing a man on a bicycle."

"Don't be silly! My dog can't ride a bicycle."

What goes tick-tock, bow-wow, tick-tock, bow-wow?

A watchdog.

What did the puppy say when it sat on sandpaper?

"Ruff!"

GIRL: "I've lost my dog."

BOY: "Why don't you put an ad in the paper?"

GIRL: "Don't be silly! My dog can't read."

Why does a dog wag its tail?

Because no one will wag it for him.

How does a sparrow with engine trouble manage to land safely?

With its sparrowchute.

What do you get if you cross a chicken with a cement mixer?

A brick-layer.

What's black and white and red all over?

A sunburned penguin.

GIRL: "I've found a penguin."

BOY: "Why don't you take it to the zoo?"

GIRL: "I took it to the zoo yesterday.
        Today we're going to the movies."

**Why don't ducks tell jokes
when they're flying?**

Because they would
quack up.

**Why do birds fly south
in the winter?**

Because it's too
far to walk.

What do you get if you cross a parrot with an alligator?

Something that bites your hand off and says, "Polly want a cracker!"

What do you call a crate of ducks?

A box of quackers.

"Mommy, mommy, I've just swallowed my harmonica!"

"Just be glad you don't play the piano."

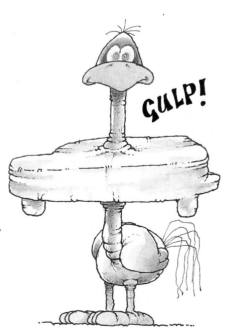

Why did the mother kangaroo scold her baby?

Because he'd been eating cookies in bed.

JIM: "What's the matter?"

TOM: "My new shoes hurt."

JIM: "That's because you've got them on the wrong feet."

TOM: "Well, they're the only feet I have."

What does an angry kangaroo do?

Get hopping mad.

SON: "Can I have another glass of water?"

FATHER: "Another? This will be your tenth!"

SON: "I know, but my room's on fire."

What did the kangaroo say when its baby disappeared?

Someone's picked my pocket!

Where do you find hippos?

It depends where you left them.

Which animal is always laughing.

A happy-potamus.

How do you tell the difference between a hippo and a banana?

If it's a hippo, you can't pick it up.

What does a hippo have if its head is hot, one foot is cold, and it sees spots?

A polka-dotted sock over its head.

Where did Napoleon keep his armies?

Up his sleevies.

What pet makes the loudest noise?

A trumpet.

Where did Humpty Dumpty leave his hat?

Humpty dumped his hat on the wall.

What has two arms, two wings, two tails, three heads, three bodies, and eight legs?

A man on a horse holding a chicken.

Mik Brown first started collecting jokes when he lived on a farm. His pigs, goats, sheep, and chickens would tell him their funniest jokes as he cleaned out their sties and pens, and even agreed to pose for his drawings. An unfortunate incident involving a chicken and a cement mixer led to Mik leaving the farm, but he continues to collect jokes from his younger children, Zoe and Izaac, and their pets—four rats, a snake, and a big black Newfoundland dog.